T0380933

Barbara Ann Mack

Balboa Press books may be ordered through booksellers or by contacting:

Balboa Press
A Division of Hay House
1663 Liberty Drive
Bloomington, IN 47403
www.balboapress.com
1 (877) 407-4847

ISBN: 978-1-9822-2239-0 (sc)
ISBN: 978-1-9822-2240-6 (e)

Library of Congress Control Number: 2019902125

Print information available on the last page.

Balboa Press rev. date: 2/22/2019

BALBOA
PRESS
A DIVISION OF HAY HOUSE

Come on in.   Catch your breath.   Quiet your mind.   Relax.

You are home.

I mean you are the home for which you have been looking.
You are love, light, complete, goodness and more.
I AM 'onenting' you to realize with me the REALITY of your being.

It feels so good.

<u>Acknowledgements</u>

I AM so thankful that

The universe cares for me.

Table of Contents

I trust in my being with all of my heart.
I release to the ethers all figuring and fear.
In all of my ways I rest in the One Mind,
And my path opens up with ease.
And my Life! takes form perfectly.

BAM! ☺

* inspired by Proverbs 3:5&6

{One} is the **Source** from which I be.

{One} is the **Life** that lives through me.

{One} is the **Mind** with which I think.

{One} is the **Love** fear is extinct.

A body **I AM** its parts all aglow.

{One} is the **Energy** that makes it all go!

2

Terms of Interest

- k(now) pronounced Know

    Knowledge realized Now — not learned, stored, habitually practiced and stale. It is fresh and of the moment — alive.

- onent pronounced onent   one syllable

    a desire to bring into expression something which I K(now) exists in the field of all possibilities,

    with an awareness of my connection to every component needed to accomplish it,

    accompanied with the good feeling that through fulfilling it, I AM expanding, enlarging, allowing, en light ening and offering increase to my sphere of influence.

- Other

    the realm of the unlabeled, open energy of eternity, the Source of all intelligent stuff.

- poWEr

    the idea that strength comes through connection.

- thankfulcating (thankful + appreciating) the action of appreciating.

- trans(form)-ulating, ulator

    new perceptions change our material experience.

I AM... I AM... I AM... this day
Reinforcing my I AM; reinforcing this NOW! way,
Contemplating in the One Mind, what One Mind might have in store
For this I AM who is open to the consciousness of mORE!

It's the bomb! It's the latest! It's the way I'm 'orienting' for—
Awesome, quantum, free form antics from the girl who lives next door.
If I can do it, You can. It's easy and it's light.
Choose to shift your way of thinking til your being feels so right.

When you're standing firmly grounded in the Light! that's Lighting you,
Infinity is the limit of what you can possibly do.
Math was not my forté but quantum physics has captured me.
It requires anOther perspective, an open mind and a release

Of the former way of thinking about space and nano parts.
Let her rip... I AM engaging on a trip which thrills my heart.
Yeah I'm out there, on the edge I feel the wind blowing my hair
As I venture into new ways to get us out of this world snares.

That's me, a quantum hotdog, exploring spaces which I find
Up above, in between, over there, and back behind.
I AM surprised at all the outcomes which are popping in to view.
Yes there's hope for this small planet— BIG solutions in the brew.

It's out there and I know it, the right path for me to choose
And I feel it as I AM doing things which humans need to do.
The Energy of Eternity moves my being with force and Light!
So I know the way to the place that I go and my steps are kept upright.

4

I k(now) the way to the place that I go,

By breathing through feelings which happen to blow.

From out of that glitch the next step comes in sight,

Perfect, fresh, rich, and freeing, on time, and just right.

It's simple and easy; you can try this at home.

Me and Alice, we do it wherever we roam.

Rabbit hole reality unfolding right here.

It's elementary dear Watson, and unequivocally clear.

We retreat from our thinking and the things we have learned,

And dive into our being where we've never been burned.

Down the hole something happens that's wonderfully strange.

All the things which were wrong somehow get changed.

So you see it's quite practical and inexpensive to boot.

Just take a deep breath and gather in your loot.

Do us a favor and get on it real soon.

The world needs its citizens being in tune.

It IS true.   It IS so.
I do 'see' what I 'see.' I do k(now) what I know.
Revisiting the past I have gathered many clues.
And they all fit together to construct anOther view.

Bits and pieces, remembered dramas form a message in my gut.
There is anOther reality. I don't belong in a human rut.
There is a Voice which is speaking. I do have eyes which can 'see.'
I AM not alone in this venture. There is a greater reality.

The signs were there to call me to a richer, lighter way
But the gravitational pull of human reason kept tripping me up day by day.
So the 'life' which was meant to be heavenly became an earthly mess
As I wandered the endless halls of my mind trapped in a thinking matrix.

But the Good never fails in its mission, working in, around, over and through
To quantumly penetrate the strongholds of the human collective point of view.
I can't make sense of all that's happened to release me from my cerebral jam
But I can tell you, this fellow sojourner, is now at home in the state of I AM.

6

In, (around), over, and ~~through~~ →

Other vibrations construct my view.
Sensing the Oneness my energy, ignites,
Drawing the completion of my `Onenting` delights.

Relaxing into Oneness, my delights can now release.
I am drinking in the nectar of Divine increase.
`Onents` which were hiding, afraid to show their face
Now Pop UP! out of nowhere in any old place!

Not to worry, my back is covered, all my ducks are in a row.
I'm receiving from the Other; what's above now shows below.
It's really quite delightful to move in Life this way.
Instead of acting all grown up, I AM is here to play.

I AM... I AM... I AM... it's so.

Kalaidescoping Godstuff the way I onent it to go.

K(now)ing that my onenting is honoring all in sight,

I snuggle with my desires while holding the compass light.

I AM... I AM... I AM... you see

Embedded in the womb of an Other reality.

My roots are richly nourished by an internal, eternal Source.

So my thoughts and words and actions can chart an Other course.

Off I go, into the 'what is,' of the sphere in which I exist

Onenting the Good and making the way for a delicious new twist.

What I used to see as opposition and barriers to my desires

Transmutes to fellow Godstuff also onenting their good to transpire.

The very people and things which I dreaded and daily got under my skin

Were now like fellow comrades and newly identified long lost kin.

Now remember this farout... revelation is emitting from deep down in my gut.

If I discount this I AM calling I'll continue in my insane human rut.

I hear you I AM... I hear you. And I do have eyes to 'see.'

I k(now) what I know and that's why I go with I AM reality.

It's light and fresh and freeing and it's so easy to implement.

I just breathe into my 'what is' and breathe out my perfect complement.

8

Sweet sounds replace the cacophony which my ears used to hear.
Lovely sights caress my eyes rather than incidents of fear.
Good thoughts fill my mind crowding out the deeds of dark.
So I dance through my days feeling free cause Life's a lark.

I AM · the Beginning · of this ever evolving scene.
I AM · the Me · who's choosing to see the good in everything.
I AM · the One · with flesh and bones who lives just up the block.
I AM · like You · journeying through bringing Light to where it's not.

I AM · the All of Everything · which could be perceived as need.
I AM · the Buck · stopping here to rest, while the solution, itself, proceeds.

I AM breathing in. I AM breathing out.
Other from within. Other all about.
I AM quieting myself so that I can really hear.
Let's go on our adventure; the runway is now clear!

In, around, over, and through,

Nothing is difficult for Other to do.
You've never really done it OR you do it e-v-e-r-y day.
Grab your magic carpet, we're goin' anOther way.

Now breathe into those engines, that's how your carpet flies.
And feel on what you're orienting; 'see' it with your eyes.
Smile into your liver. Taste it on your tongue.
We're quantumly connecting with the awesome poWEr of One.

Bless your `NOW` surroundings, appreciate your 'hood,
Cause that's 'the' way of Other to see the `NOW` as good.
that warmth is surely drawing all the things which you will need
So the pieces come together quite easily indeed.

It's fun to take up flying. It's the only way to go.
Just fire up those engines with awareness from your soul.

I AM... I AM... I AM... shifting and shaking the forms.
bending and broadening the norms.
feeling into Other for good.
skipping over the understood.

Immediate gratification `that's what I like to feel!
So I breathe into my Other mind, calling out the Other with zeal.
I just can't wait to get started, feeling good and better and best.
I can do it with my Other thoughts. I can do it right Now with zest!

I AM taking off quite happily from the country called What Has Been.
I'm engaging the Other reality and entering the land of I Can!
Zero to great in just seconds— No way to That's Sweet in a snap.
The G-force can be a little startling, so be sure to buckle your strap.

Are you fighting your way on the freeway or about to give the toilet a flush?
Which ever of the two is more stinky the Other can clear it in a rush.
I don't mean to be irreverent, overly graffic, or down right crude
But the odor of some of these feelings, about these thoughts, does color our moods.

So let's choose some delicious new thoughts so we can feel a delightful new way.
Then the odor will morph into a fragrance which we can now proudly display!
Breathe into Other for suggestions of your next, best, good.
Then exhale your new thinking from beyond the understood.

"Strange," "Are you kidding?" "Ridiculous!" is what your ego may taunt.
But trust the I AM with[in] you, to guide in ALL that you `onent.
Should turbulence of contrasting 'what is' cause a bumpy, unpleasant spell
Remember that strap low and firm on your lap and smile cause you know all is well.

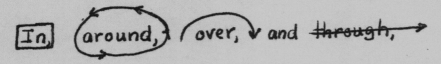

In, (around,) over, ↓ and ~~through,~~ →

Other and Life can rock a sweet tune.
They're jammin' and I'm jivin' cause I can't resist the beat.
The energy of ALL being —— it just gets me on my feet.

I'm relaxing in my shoulders; it's releasing from my back,
The responsibility of continuing a constant plan of attack.
I breathe into that k(now)ing. I think I'll just rest here.
It feels <u>so</u> good, this notion, of an Other healing sphere.

I'm a ragdoll - always smiling - there's no need to change my face,
Cause wherever this ragdoll is going, Other is rockin' \out/ that happenin' space.
You could also say I'm full of It everywhere, all over [in]side.
But you <u>can't</u> say this doll is a dummy to trust the intelligent action of Life!

I AM fresh, flowing, flippy free.
Come out being. Come be with me.
We'll sashe' through the things to do.
Let's smile and skip and laugh some too.

I'm gonna wash these thoughts right out of your head,
Limitation, lack, dramatizations of dread.
I'm gonna fill your mind with things that are best —
More and plenty, sharing, doing filled with zest.

To do the job rightly, I'll bring in the big guns —
Life and Other hum together as they get the job done.
Pros and buddies they work smoothly and thoroughly too.
In and out, quick and easy and the price is right for you.

We never met a predicament we couldn't 'see' through.
You're NOT a tough cookie; We've got your number too.
You've been figuring and chewing on the same old fat.
There are Other thoughts to consider — a whole NEW vat.

So you're weary and you're worn out by your nagging, nail biting thoughts?
Welcome to our trans(form)ulator. We're offering feel good plots.
Put your feet up. Take a load off. The buck stops bucking right here,
Because the ENERGY of ALL BEING is now I AMMING loud and clear.

There's something in the air. No, it's stirring from in me.
No there's something flowing in and out indescriminately.
It's delicious, warm, and onederful; as it washes through my mind.
Well, I 'see' you've tasted Other and you're liking what you find.

A day which seemed too difficult heading toward despair
Just ka-chinged into Light with hope, hopping everywhere.
Now I think it only fitting, that you offer up some 'thanks.'
Thank you, I AM. I AM thankful that I AM the end of angst.

I AM... I AM... I AM... I say.
Come on! all the Universe — Come \out/ and play!
It's safe. I love you. I like you a lot.
Together we'll adventure and enjoy what we've got.

I AM... I AM... I AM right here
Engaging the people who aren't to come near.
I'm beaming well-being with all of my heart
Broadcasting we're ` ONE ⌐ to every last part.

I AM... I AM... I AM... on a hill,
Singing and dancing expressing at will,
Releasing to the ethers good feelings from [in]side.
Welcome all creation; join in with the vibe.

Come on, let's bring it! Give it up! Let it fly!
Sound it out! Fill the heavens! Blow your trumpet! Blast the sky!
Feel your being. Love your body. Hug the 'what is' of this day.
Cause it's flowing and it's moving and it's morphing a Good way.

HALLELUJAH! It is happening. It's unfolding and I 'see.'
That I'm dancing in the middle and belonging WHILE being me.
I'm relaxing and I'm smiling and relating and feeling good.
As I'm living \out/ I AM... in my NOW neighborhood.

I do not come from here

My beginning is from before

Though I walk through space and time,

My reality is abundantly mORE

For a season I seemed existing

under the lure of this world's law.

Forever grateful I am for awakening

to my Source who fills me with awe.

My purpose I think is quite simple,

to live what I AM where I be.

Skipping along in unbreakable oneness

allowing Life to open up with ease.

I k(now) the way to the place that I go

By sporting I AM... all over the globe.

In my bed or at my sink,

I acknowledge I AM... before I start to think.

I AM... I AM... I AM... right here —

Beaming from my spaces I love me instead of fear.

I open my eyes to the Kingdom inside

And ready myself for a real sweet ride.

With my I AM... glasses firmly sitting on my nose,

I 'see' daily happenings as friends instead of foes.

I welcome the 'what is' which is buzzing around my head,

To become a cherished visitor bringing light! instead of dread.

And the magic starts to happen in an instant... in a wink.

A wonderful scent is flowing from something which used to stink!

Transmutation seems complex but I explained it all quite clear.

The things I used to hate become the ones I 'see' as dear.

16

I K(now) the way to the place that I go,

By getting what I need from down the rabbit hole.

It's really so convenient and reasonable to find

That I carry all I onen't-right now- it's nestled in my mind.

Now, you won't 'learn' this from guru's or from those who love to teach

Because you K(now) it through your being; it's always been in your reach.

So why am I going over what's already to you Known?

Well, perhaps you don't remember and in the world you feel alone.

Let's you and I sit down right now and consider our current state.

Is it based on all we see outside — lack, fear, and shades of hate?

Here I am a fellow earthling facing the same things that you do,

But I have a different outlook and anOther point of view.

It comes from the *light* we both have [in]side guiding us through our day.

We trust what we K(now) and that's how we go making choices along the way.

So let's think on that <u>base</u>, not making a <u>case</u> from all that appears awry.

And we'll be strangely stable, calm, clear and quite able to accomplish whatever we try.

I K(now) the way to the place that I go

By speaking what I 'see' in the human collective show.

As the dramas are reported, I 'see' anOther thing;

It's the absolute Truth peeking through the forms again.

(Drama)

He did this. She did that. Whatever will I do?

I'm confused. It's not fair. That's craziness from my view.

I just don't Know. It's _so_ hard. It takes _so_ long to make things right.

Don't you see? Come join with me in this ugly unfolding plight.

My friends ask me to save for them an ever sinking ship.

But I 'see' a boat, which is firmly afloat, if they could only get a grip

On the Way of Good, working through the _what is_, presented to them each day.

And gladly join in the 'positive_ with|in\ as it's waiting to come out and play.

(The Absolute Truth)

I love him. I love her. I k(now) exactly what to do.

I see clearly and it's good for them to express their point of view.

I _do_ k(now). It's _so_ easy and in a twinkle things CAN change.

Yes, I 'see' and join happily in the dance upon this plane.

There _IS_ anOther reality paralleling our various scenes.

So, I speak up about the _Good_ and _Truth_ I know that REALLY reigns.

At first it seems unnatural and unacceptable to my peers

But in time they 'see' the validity of that which quiets all their fears.

I AM breathing into Other. I'm looking forward to this day.

Living is a piece of cake, when I 'see' it an Other-fangled way.

My organs are tuning up. My cells are tweaking too

To the frequency of perfection, easing my mind, so all systems are cool.

Though trillions, we move as One; I used to 'think' we were two,

My ego ordering my body along as if it was too stupid to move.

NOW, I know it is intelligent, as is ALL the stuff around.

ALL the parts are filled with the buzz of Life, just waiting to hear the sound.

I 'see' you. {ka-ching} we're together. Together, we're One Fine machine.

Let by-gones now be by-gones. Let's move ahead with a slate that's clean.

And now I'll slip into Other — it's a way that's never been done —

One that's light and fresh and freeing with adventure — just enough — to be fun.

So I breathe into my body, into the space that has never been used.

And I ease on down the Other road in a light and happy mood.

I AM now aware of my body. I AM connecting with the intelligence stored there.

I AM realizing the full abundance, of ALL I onent is first found in here.

I AM breathing into my potential and releasing old stuff I don't need.

I AM love. I AM light. I'm abundant. Did I mention I'm also complete?

I AM grateful and newly connected to the people and space around me.

I AM renewed, relaxed, and ready for the dance of Life I choose to 'see'.

I 'see' you, is my new mantra. Namaste', it works too.

The exact words really don't matter so much. It's the vibration which sculpts

the dance tune.

19

I AM breathing into Other. I AM opening my eyes
To the world of my creating which is bigger than the skies.
It's deeper than my longings, so much richer. It's now called `onents.
Six impossible things <u>before</u> breakfast are now here ✓ not wishful thoughts.

Breathing, yes, I'm breathing. I AM breathing into ONE.
What is hard and quite undoable, for me, is said and dONE.
My yoke it <u>feels</u> so easy; my burden, well, it's light.
It's a pleasure to bring into expression the things which fit just right.

I 'see' it with my Other eyes and <u>feel</u> it with my soul,
Until it makes the transition from invisible to it's new role.
I can't rationally explain it. I'm just telling you it's true.
If you warmly welcome your own `onents, they'll surely come home to you.

Just remember it's always fﬂowing, all of the matter, all of the time.
Rest into the rhythm — 'see' and speak of it as Divine.
Listen, for the music your I AM will surely hear.
Then, dance the dance of living through it's stages and consciousness tiers.

I AM breathing into Other — taking a break from my thinking mind.
I'M releasing, relaxing, resting when I AM shocked at what I find!
Amongst love and light and plenty, lots of space and Other neat stuff,
There AM I. Yes, its ME. I AM present. I AM Other sure enough.

I'm dumbfounded, incredulous, speechless — my jaw drops as I blankly stare
Into the realm of Other and the potential, potentialities there.
I AM quiet. I AM still. I AM peaceful. I AM realizing my interspheric space.
Don't worry about me Scotty. I can beam myself back to home base.

I AM safe. I AM sound. I AM physical. I AM real and this really is true.
In the stillness I clearly do 'see' it — this totally awesome, quantum worldview.
Then comes a calling that begging question, How, then, shall I NOW live?
So I turn to my in house counsel asking Awareness its answer to give.

Let's see. Jesus, Ghandi and Methusalah would answer that question the same.
Keep walking, keep loving, keep breathing and you surely will achieve your aim.
Enlightenment, lightens your understanding as your unique journey unfolds.
So if this "ah-ha" is really genuine, a delightful direction should simply be exposed.

What a relief I feel in my fibers — my soul, it can still dance and sing.
As I breathe again into Other a certain lightness that thought does bring.
I AM Now aware of anOther way and I AM Now Other in form view.
So as long as I move in Awareness, I will k(now) exactly what to do.

21

About <u>any</u>thing and <u>every</u>thing I'm onenting NOW so much,
I AM breathing into Other. I AM breathing on my hunch,
That in Other is the Mother Lode just waiting to be got.
Done and finished, quick and easy, It's now here where it was not!

That's the way I like it, with some mystery involved.
I just hold the compass lightly til the Universe is resolved
To the vibration of my desire no matter what it's for.
Other has it covered at the Infinite Possibilities Store.

What is it that you're onenting? What desires fill your heart?
Let go of why it can't be and let Other do it's part.
Dare to **feel** the onenting of what you know you'll surely get.
Then smile into your liver. You have cast a winning bet.

And until it's manifested in this form world that we live,
Let Other show you Its way to authentically give.
24/7. It's a journey of ascending light.
You might even forget your onenting cause true giving is such a delight.

It's a blast to join the party Life that Other is offering you.
Bring your friends and foes and family and some interesting misfits too.
Anything goes, all is allowed, no one is left out in the cold.
The miracle of I AM trans(form)ing is one that never gets old.

22

I breathe away my thinking. I exhale what I've learned.

I give thanks for the stuff I AM full of... pristine soil never been turned.

In that fertile, fallow potential I can establish Other roots.

The Energy of Eternity then empoWErs those sprouting shoots.

I feel the energy buzzing. It is electrifying the air.

I smell a fragrance wafting. It IS happening I declare!

Assertive yet allowing this Some thing is Onederfully strange.

The Energy of Eternity easily perfectly brings about change.

It's not partial to a doctrine, personal history or color of skin.

It doesn't harbor resentments or rigid judgments of what has been.

It flows unimpeded through the wooing, welcoming one.

Who `onents` simple, sacred Good to perfectly be said and dONE.

That's me. I breathe into my body. "THAT'S mE!" I say it out loud.

I AM... I AM... I AM beaming — brightly being without a doubt.

I AM rich. I AM light. I AM freeing. I AM pure and fresh and clean.

I AM ONE with the Energy of Eternity and I AM loving the REAL me.

I'm One with the Other; all here is well.
Yes, I'm One with the Other — I'm so happy to tell
That I'm thinking on all that's good. It's forming as we speak.
Dancing — expanding on the canvas inside me.

Wonders and healings, common days filled with meaning,
Plenty and more than the talk of each day.
Loving and laughter, my companions everafter,
K(now)ing ever flowing surely making my way.

K(now)ing ever flowing surely making my way.

I am Safe.

ALL is Well I AM happy to tell you
And getting better with each breath that I breathe.
It is EASY to breathe into my spaces.
More and plenty is fun to receive.

On the court I 'see' lots of choices
As my thoughts are dribbling down.
And I hear a myriad of voices.
Go this way. No that way. Try around.
The noise, the crowd, the confusion
Which many times has sabataged me
Now loses its power of assertion
As I choose what I 'onent' quietly.

Former thinking fed on the drama, the conflict, taking up sides
To keep my adrenaline flowing so I would think that I was really living life.
I'm so happy to wake up to It's easy. Life is good and I'm shaping the plan
As I feel into my body, choose from my spaces and trust my I AM.

The I AM is perfect energy. I AM is now flowing as me.
It feeds, it cleanses, it's healing. It's directing my next step - my next lead.
I AM always does the next best thing for me and those in my sphere.
So dare to feel your own onenting because it's/we're definitely happening here.

23

Have you heard of the Tower of Babel? I deal with it every day.
The minute I start to quiet myself, legion voices cry out, "No way!"
Not to worry or even get flustered, I just breathe into the spaces of me.
As I acknowledge the peace which I AM inside, the rabble rousers quickly recede.

The quiet, quietly gathers itself while my spaces a temple do form.
I AM my own house of worship. I AM a thing to be adorned.
I always carry it [in] me. I AM therefore holy [in]side.
If I choose to honor my [in]side spaces, then the holiness shows up\out/side.

Here it is, that Big Hairy Monster— a screeching, demanding urgent need.
But Awareness also shows its face whispering quietly, "You KNOW you CAN breathe."
And the drama dramatically dissipates to a thing I NOW can wield.
As I consciously navigate the 'what is' until smooth sailing it does yield.

Not to worry or even get flustered, I just breathe into the spaces of me.
As I acknowledge the I AM [in] myself, the unique steps happily release,
Out of thin air the world would term it but I 'see' anOther way.
The spaces are full of every thing just waiting to come into play.

The players are all agreeable, eagerly orienting to play their bit.
To be involved in the thing I AM 'seeing', adding their own special twist.
Through my 'seeing', I'm actually gathering a pick-up team of sorts
To manifest my orents and desires until the finished product results.

HOW can that be you doubtfully ask me? A gentle smile forms on my lips.
I'm remembering my similar disbelief as I've journeyed along my own trip.
Focus on what really interests YOU — the appetite generated from [in]side.
Then follow the path YOU are 'seeing' until at your destination you arrive.

I AM an I AM; you are one too.
We're both on the journey. Now isn't that cool?
I AM quite dramatic — you're not of the same bent.
Still, we're traveling buddies on this road of enlightenment.

Just wondering how you're doing with your I AMMing this fine day.
I know that good is happening ALL the time, in every way.
You can't stop it, this flow of energy — flowing here, flowing there.
The Energy of Eternity — it's making light e-v-e-r-y-w-h-e-r-e.

In the darkest, loneliest corners, it's just waiting to be seen.
Until it is acknowledged — then it shines like anything.
I know it because it happens in my house inside of me.
I'm just minding my own business and it happens naturally.

I think about a some one — well — like you who comes to mind.
And I'm thankful for the Truth which only you could help me find.
No one else could do the job, you showed up on the right day,
To be who you are, to say what you said and to do it in your unique way.

We do it for each other. We're just onederful we two.
Hey, I think there's a BIG message in this rhyme for me and you.
Together we get more light! then by going it alone.
Thank you traveling buddy together we're in the ZONE.

I AM... I AM... I AM... It's true.
Is the common denominator for me And for you.
You are an I AM and I AM one too.
We are ALL I AM's in this world, at this school.

In our homes, on the street, at the mall — hangin' out
We are ALL I AM's — I AMMING about.
Expressing I AM in our current chosen way.
This is the I AM, I AM showing you today.

Appearances are shifting; attitudes can change.
But there is a constant factor which does remain the same.
I AM always an I AM; the other is an I AM too.
So focus on that I AM that is breathing through both of you.

Step up to be the first one to think it in your mind.
Soon those thoughts will cause actions and you'll be surprised to find,
That YOU started something radical by choosing this simple way,
Of honoring your I AM as you honor the other's today.

Seeing the Good today and each week,
What is normal to me, to others is Greek.
It's building and boosting and blessing my sphere.
So we're all getting more in our own atmosphere.

I AM... I AM... I AM... it's true,
A 'see'er of Good for me And for you.
Feeling the Good in the dramas of the norm,
I 'see' the Good in our stumbling forms.

Fleshing it out we fashion a bouquet
Of a Onederful fragrance in public display.
Gracing the air where a stench once stood,
We're raising the quality of our neighborhood.

So you see it IS practical for times such as these
To welcome the Good in our daily routines.
It improves our health, our economy, our fate
To honor the worth of our beingness state.

I AM... I AM... I AM... this minute.
Let awareness take this event and spin it—
From my helpless, hopeless frame of mind
To the surreal reality I K(now) I can find.

I feel into my body and breathe into it too,
Creating a bubble of awareness in which the solution does brew.
Time loses its insistence, limitation is revealed as fake.
So I do whatever I'm doing realizing my I AM state.

Meanwhile — the Universe is hopping, multi-tasking and coming through
With a perfectly harmonious answer for the obstacle that I viewed,
Spinning a fairy tale ending to a frenetic human scene.
I receive it all quite gladly, giving thanks in everything.

But from where did I receive it? From where did it all come?
Out of the Good which exists within my k(now)n Kingdom.
The shelves are full and overflowing, the possibilities are out of sight
Waiting to be manifested, fulfilling my focused delight.

I AM... I AM... I AM... came through.
As it happens through me, it can happen through you.

I AM... I AM... I AM... this day,
'Seeing' my events in a whimsical way.
Observing them turn and switch about,
Til the perfect result comes easily out.

I'm tempted to manipulate and fret and try,
But awareness keeps whispering, "You're okay." by and by.
So I go with the flow and trust what I 'hear',
Allowing my body to transmute all I fear.

I feel into my body as the experiences brew,
And I'm carried along perfectly all-the-way through.
When it's questioned, "What has happened?" at the end of the day,
I just smile ↝ as I put my magic carpet away.

I AM... I AM... I AM... today.

I AM I AMMING in a Now kind of way.

It's good. It's practical. It _feels_ so right to me.

To ride my magic carpet in this world so normally.

Awareness, my conductor, calls out "ALL ABOARD!"

So my senses, take their places, at the windows and the doors.

Checking out the sights, and taking in the views

they gush amongst each other, "Oh, it's wonderful. Aahh... ooo!"

But not long after take-off...

Going to the library or chopping onions at my sink,

Stuff happens which triggers me to follow my old instincts.

Here it comes, that dreaded fearing, churning, rising in my gut.

How the heck did I think I could be happy; I'm still in the same stinkin' rut!

"Is that so?" asks my conductor. Are you sure your facts are straight?

Is there something you are overlooking in this ruling about your fate?

Take a breath.... exhale stillness. Sit with Other for a while.

So you can help, your misguided senses, to 'see' what they know, in I AM style.

Oh... I 'see' an Other feeling stretching, growing as I chop.

It's the presence of my being expanding, enlarging — I'm going to POP!

With the JOY of really experiencing the wind blow through my hair

As I ride my magic carpet in this world everywhere.

I AM... I AM... I AM... it's clear.
The I AM reality leaves nothing to fear.
I 'see' what I AM and I like what I 'see'.
What's not to like about I AM and me?

Well...

Moving in form life I sometimes get riled—
Reacting to other forms instead of living I AM style.
Forgetting that it's now, I act out some past scene
Based on old, stored conflict and unresolved, revolving themes.

But...

Awareness is ever present always willing to save the day.
I can -STOP- whatever I'm doing - and request an Other way.
A possibility which seemed nonexistent until I put out a call,
Now presents itself non dramatically, as if it were nothing at all!

So...

I like what I 'see', when I'm looking, for something easy and good.
And I like being positive and happy, in my very, own, neighborhood.
I AM affecting the world all over every where,
As I main stream the Other vibration in the human collective sphere.

I AM... I AM... I AM... this day,
Thinking of Love in an Other kind of way.
Enjoying the "Now" of my many relationships
I can quantumly love deeply without even getting a grip!

I AM sending out my love, to those who come to mind,
Without the need to receive from them, a likewise gift in kind.
It feels _so_ good releasing that warmth and caring through me —
Why I'm just a walking love machine filled to over capacity.

In form life, we think loving is shown by our "sacrificial" good deeds,
But actually, in those actions, we often find some rotten seeds,
Of future expectations on the unsuspecting souls,
Who accept the gift, unaware of the rift, driving us to fill a hole.

Today I AM so thankful, appreciating and fully in(form)ed,
That I can EASILY love e-v-e-r-y-o-n-e and that's the REAL norm!
It's _NOT_ hard, no exceptions. It's EASY, simple and clear.
Read my lips, fellow Earthlings, the end of our hating is here.

I AM... I AM... I AM... this day
Thinking about money in an Other kind of way.
I often _feel_ overwhelmed or that I'm in a financial mess.
But the Universe sees it differently. It finds no need to stress.

If I think on the cost of living, monthly bills, or outstanding loans
I'm dragged into the drama of the human collective moans.
From Kansas City to Calcutta — in Bejing you can hear the cry.
There isn't enough. Life on Earth, here, is rough. Why... oh why... oh why?

All the while the Universe is smiling, quietly waiting for the wails to subside.
It's all quite simple. It clucks to me. Let's look at the 'what is' [IN]side.
It's a Kingdom of _Light_ and of plenty — ~~loving~~, sharing and mor℮ than enough
In this Land of I Can, Life is good and I AM always 'onenting' and receiving the right stuf.

Hey, what's the postage for a letter to Calcutta? What's the rate for one to Bejing?
I've just got to tell them how good it _feels_ to think on all the right things!
There's plenty... It's easy... I know it... That mantra could bring what's [IN] out!
Holy Smokes I forgot Kansas City! I can't wait to give them a shout.

So, if you, by chance, _feel_ downhearted, about your current state,
Breathe —— [IN] to your own Kingdom and release an Other fate.
No one can do it for you. You've got it. You are _already_ whole.
Just breathe [IN] to that engine and let the good times roll.

34

Have you met my pet elephant? It's REAL and big and gray.
Though I only feed it peanuts, it never wanders away.
Sometimes it is invisible; Other times it's in my face.
That teddy bear of an elephant goes with me ALL OVER the place.

When I find myself angry, all I can see is gray,
Because that dog gone elephant encompasses me from every which way!
On the thick, tough skin between those wirey hairs sticking out —
It's like a big movie screen with motion pictures moving about.

There I AM smack in my drama, creating, scheming a nefarious plot.
When a Voice calls, "STOP THE ACTION! Let's look for an Other shot."
I AM startled by the intrusion — dumbfounded — but oh, so relieved.
Why — my thoughts were diabolically doing stuff that's not I AM me.

As I collapse into Oneness, my absolute choice of faire,
I realize the hate and ugliness completely vanished into — NOT-here.
It's over, finished, done with. All I can smell is the scent of a rose.
And that's why I love my pet elephant for saving me in times such as those.

My yoke is incredibly EASY;
My burden is a happy delight!
I AM breezing along Life's highway
ALWAYS doing the action that's right.

I'm a pleasure to have as a sibling,
A friend, confidante or a muse.
I AM light. I AM loving. I AM helpful.
I AM perfect for any old use.

I love the ...(your name).... I AM seeing.
I AM bright. I AM savvy. I AM kind.
I AM perfect for any occasion.
Another one you'll never find.

I AM...ONE harmoniously, happenin' fleet
         strong, poWErful and onederfully replete
         as I happily, dynamically translate from the Greek —
         Life is good. So are we. I love me. This now is sweet.

         I AM sweet. I AM kind,
         without fail or even tryin'.
         I AM rich. I AM free
         Like a winsom summer breeze.
         It is easy. It is NOW
         As I quantumly allow,
         My connection with perfection
         Breathing out my form direction.
         I AM REAL. It is great!
         ALL of Life! I appreciate.
         I AM flowing, flowing, flowing,
         As I REALIZE my knowing.

I AM safe. I AM sound. I AM happy.
ALL of EVERYTHING permeates me.
I AM resting in the flow — I AM One is my M.O.
So all I onent shows uprightly AND easily.
      I AM... I AM... I AM... resonating
      With the Universe as it smiles on our frequent consternating,
      Through my onenting, transmuting, and playful verbalating —
      I DO know. Yes, I see and I'm filled with thankfulcating.
I love you Life. I love you. I love you. I really do.
And the more we play together the more other will come into view.
I do take other seriously, but I just have to chuckle too
Cause it feels so good to be doing the thing that I was meant to do.

I AM... I AM... I AM... this day
Feeling not so good. Feeling NOT okay.
Doubting cleverly clouding the ALL IS WELL which I once spoke
Life is good. So are we. I love me also fading. Was it all a joke?

Quick the trans(form)ulator. Hurry! Right NOW! Don't wait!
We're losing 'light' consciousness. We're losing the I AM state.
Breathe deeply into your body. Breathe quietly focusing there.
Keep breathing-breathing-breathing until breathing is all you can hear.

Hello. Can you hear me? You have been placed under my care.
I'll be monitoring your case closely. My name is Dr. Aware.
I AM available 24/7 to help you realize your positive state.
Complete recovery is quite possible-in fact your future looks just great.

Continue breathing, breathing, breathing. Use your body to even conditions out.
Your stored thoughts, released old emotions which triggered dark responses to come about
These things can sometimes happen, out of the blue, taking you by surprise.
But if you remain under my care, I guaranty we'll 'see' more light.

This treatment is REVOLUTIONARY yet it's as old as Methusalah too.
Sages throughout the ages have touted the Awareness School.
It's simple, cheap, and e-a-s-y, highly effective and cuts to the chase.
You are unfolding salvation when you are moving in an I AM state.

I always carry a trans(form)ulator as I make my way through life.
So I can breathe my way through circumstances which aren't feeling just right.
I AM feeling increasingly better. I k(now) I AM free of dis-ease.
And I AM speaking it OUT to the Universe so all creation can join with me.

I AM breathing into Other with ALL the Other I have got.

I AM trusting in that Other to bring more Other \out/ of that.

I AM living Other reality, Other gaining more ground each day.

I AM grounding my form in Other because I love this Other way.

I AM breathing, breathing, breathing, resting, relaxing— It feels good!

I AM releasing through my breathing thoughts on Life MIS understood.

I AM breathing, breathing, breathing inviting lightness to take hold.

I AM breathing, breathing, breathing `orienting` light to be my mold.

I AM breathing, breathing, breathing smiling and feeling \out/ my thanks.

I AM breathing, breathing, breathing happily releasing phantom angst.

I AM breathing, breathing, breathing breathing outcomes to soothe my soul.

I AM breathing, breathing, breathing— resonating with the whole.

I AM breathing <u>with</u> a body, <u>on</u> this planet, <u>in</u> my sphere.

I AM breathing quietly bringing expanding light to conditions here.

I AM breathing where I AM being; I AM FULL of perfect light!

Through my breathing, I AM freeing forms just like me to take <u>THEIR</u> flight.

Breathing, yes I'm breathing, breathing deeply into me.
I AM releasing to the ethers whining, demanding phantom needs.
My body exhales its thank you as it melts into my chair.
My mind, it sits down too — taking a moment of laissez-faire.

ALL my form parts take a siesta. It's ALL quiet in my frame.
Every body part onents its respite. Everyone onents it the same.
I can't tell you _what_ they're doing when I'm doing nothing else.
But I k(now) that it's trans(form)ing for my well-being and body health.

Do yourself a favor. Try it out. Give it a shot.
Breathing deeply, releasing worry just might cure the ills YOU'VE got.
I AM really feeling better. I've been doing it awhile.
I AM replacing frenetic attitudes with a whole body smile.

I waken to our {one}ness.
My soul K(now)s I belong.
{One} hums throughout my being.
Safe and loved I AM at home.

{One} vibrates through my body.
Thoughts dance to correspond.
Things manifest out of nothing!
And I rest while its all d{one}.

I 'see' the Joy of living;
It's e-a-s-y when I'm {one}.
The world is out to help me.
Thank you.   Thank you. I respond.

I k(now) the way to the place that I go,

By picturing my steps the way I `orient´ them to flow.

Wooing the invisible to form in my space,

As I lovingly welcome it home at my place.

Feeling the `Joy´ as I see it so clear,

I beam it from nowhere to manifest here.

I'm so glad that you're here; I'm so glad that you came.

Let's enJoy´ one anOther in this synchronistic frame.

Aaahh! My yoke Is so easy; my burden Is light.

Right perception shows Life is fitting just right.

So I rest in my `Joy´ and express ⟨out — the good.

And the flow is increased in my neighborhood.

Expanding and growing from [in]side of me,

It's the fruit from the Field of All Possibilities.

In, around, over and through,
My ringing vibrations recruit the crew.
Catching the vibe, the ones ignite
Moved by the unction of their heart's delight.

Sensing that "Something" which is calling in the crew,
A response is required from out of the blue.
So rich and captivating is this light, freeing song
That the ones being awakened can't wait to dance along.

Trusting the Mother Matrix to engage the perfect find,
I relax with my desires and I ` JoY in peace of mind,
Which surges the transmission through a nonresistant sphere.
The Universe multi-tasking with nothing, nowhere to interfere.

Right now as I'm musing, sitting here, in this chair,
I'm shaking up the matter all over _everywhere!_
Kalaidescoping my desires in the fluid realm of mind,
I can mix and match, paste and patch, completing my design.

I have all that I `onent´ because the Universe knows
Where its arms and hands are swinging —
What's squishing round its toes.

The God stuff of creation is made only of One Kind.
So the atoms, molecules and elements work together all the time.
What a party! What a blowout! The vibrations are supreme.
Life! it's happening — so harmoniously in everyday with everything.

The Stuff that I am made of, and the Stuff that's over there —
It's all universal Godstuff, just vibrating there or here.
I hum out my desires as they come to be made known,
The Universe delivers; it's only caring for its own.
And likewise the Godstuff, beingness, that I would call... me,
Gladly serves the other Godstuff light hearted and happily.

It's moving and it's flowing all the Godstuff all around.
As I call for Some I'm `onenting´ it easily can be found.
Peaceful, present, ready. I `heard´ this all inside.
As I listened, I remembered. You know, I knew it all the time.
I `see´ by looking inside, what is Truth and what's of worth,
Then I join the party happily for the Godstuff here on earth.

Index

About the Author

Barbara (Fountain) Mack was born in rural Iowa. She received an Interdisciplinary Degree in the Humanities from the University of Northern Iowa. In her junior year she submitted a term paper entitled "Pleasing the Self," in which she synthesized a semester's class information into an inter related, multi-level view point. Her professors were amazed, and her curiosity was piqued at the possibility and benefit of this interdisciplinary view of common life experiences.

In the next years, working for a nonprofit, career education organization in metropolitan New Jersey, she garnered experience from interfacing with politics and fund raising, corporate power structures, school systems: rural to inner city and image building at a personal and professional level. Later, as a dorm supervisor for seven years at a religious institution, she added multi-national relationships as well as employee and student mediation. For more than a year Barbara engaged in life studies for inmates at a maximum security women's prison.

Barbara has always journaled, categorized, philosophized and re-adjusted her world view, reaching for a positive yet realistic outlook. Good Bless You percolated out of her life experiences. Her second book, I AM, follows as a practical companion.

She and her husband, Ted, and their teenage daughters, Martha Anne and Susan, live in sunny, southern California with their dog, Jack, and their cat, Mr. Daisy.

Printed in the United States
By Bookmasters